THE WILD GIANT PANDA

BY SANDRA WIDENER

Harcourt

Orlando   Boston   Dallas   Chicago   San Diego

Visit *The Learning Site!*

www.harcourtschool.com

Have you ever seen a wild giant panda? Only one animal has that kindly face and those fluffy black hind legs.

Wild giant pandas are not like
black bears. Giant pandas eat
bamboo. Black bears do not. Pandas
do not hibernate or walk on their
hind legs like black bears do.

Wild giant pandas live high in
the forests of China. About 1,000
of them live in the wild in China.

Wild giant pandas in China
spend ten or more hours every day
finding food. Wild pandas eat one
kind of food—bamboo.

Wild giant pandas must eat more than fifty pounds of bamboo in a day. No wonder the giant panda spends so much time looking for food!

Each wild giant panda needs lots of land to find that much bamboo. Maybe that is why they don't like other pandas around.

Once wild pandas find bamboo,
they grind it with their big teeth.
Giant pandas eat almost every
part of the bamboo. Very little is
left behind.

When giant pandas are born, they are tiny. A grown giant panda can weigh 220 pounds, but a newborn panda weighs only a few ounces!

A wild giant panda mother is very kind. She keeps her tiny infant in a special pouch during the first few months.

When a young panda is about eight months old, both mother and child know the little panda is ready to leave the pouch. The young panda looks for its own bamboo to eat.

Thousands of years ago, many Chinese people thought that wild giant pandas were special. Even then, pandas were very rare. People in China thought that pandas brought good luck.

Today many people are trying
to protect giant pandas in the wild
in China.

The people of China give giant
pandas to other countries as a sign
of friendship. There are giant
pandas in zoos all over the world.

People who see giant pandas in zoos love these animals from China. People like to see giant pandas as much as lions and tigers.

People who see the giant panda in the zoo may want to help save pandas in the wild. They can help make the giant panda safe in the wilds of China.